The Wisdom of Women

The
Wisdom of
Women

Selected and with an Introduction by
CAROL SPENARD LaRUSSO

THE CLASSIC WISDOM COLLECTION
NEW WORLD LIBRARY
SAN RAFAEL, CALIFORNIA

8/95

The Classic Wisdom Collection
Published by New World Library
58 Paul Drive, San Rafael, CA 94903

Cover design: Greg Wittrock
Text design: Nancy Benedict
Typography: Wilsted & Taylor

Library of Congress Cataloging-in-Publication Data

The Wisdom of women / selected and with an introduction
by Carol Spenard LaRusso.
        p. cm. — (The Classic wisdom collection)
    Includes bibliographical references and index.
    ISBN 1-880032-09-0 (acid-free paper).
    1. Women—Quotations. 2. Quotations, English.
I. LaRusso, Carol Spenard, 1935–   . II. Series.
PN6081.5 W48 1992   92-17602
082'.082—dc20   CIP

First printing, November 1992
ISBN 1-880032-09-0
Printed in the U.S.A. on acid-free paper

Gift/JS

To my mother, with love

Contents

Publisher's Preface

Life is an endless cycle of change. We and our world will never remain the same.

Every generation has difficulty relating to the previous generation; even the language changes. The child speaks a different language than the parent.

It seems almost miraculous, then, that certain voices, certain books, are able to speak to not only one, but many generations beyond them. The plays and poems of William Shakespeare are still relevant today—still capable of giving us goose bumps, still entertaining, disturbing, and profound. Shakespeare is the writer who, in the English language, defines the word *classic*.

There are many other writers and thinkers who, for a great many reasons, can be considered classic, for they withstand the test of time. We want to present the best of them to you in the New World Library Classic Wisdom Collection, the thinkers who, even though they lived many years ago, are still relevant and important in today's world for the enduring words of wisdom they created, words that should forever be kept in print.

The Wisdom of Women is a special book in this collection, an eclectic gathering of the writings of women from diverse cultures, past and present. We are proud to present this tribute to the profundity and power of women.

Shakti Gawain
Marc Allen
New World Library

Introduction

The Wisdom of Women is a collection of selected short passages from the writings and sayings of women from around the world, those of today and yesterday. Writers, artists, musicians—young and old, sophisticated and simple, famous and not-so-famous. Doctors, lawyers, scientists, political activists, entrepreneurs—daughters, mothers, wives—all share their thoughts on war and peace, the future, life and love, freedom, family, the spiritual life. Through the tapestry of their varied backgrounds, cultures, and their time in history, we trace the common thread of the feminine principle— the recurring patterns of feeling, connection, and communication.

The history of the world is a history of women, though for much of it they were the "second" sex, the "other." This book is a celebration of their power and wisdom, their incredible ability to prevail and survive in largely patriarchal societies. The power of women has long been covert: "The hand that rocks the cradle rules the world," though, unfortunately, this has not been true enough. As we move into the twenty-first century, however, woman's power is increasingly overt—in the workplace, boardroom, on campus, in government, the arts, education, and in professions and careers that were once the exclusive bastions of men.

I believe that women, and the feminine principle, have contributed the lion's share to staving off that most hideous of destinies, nuclear war. The talent of women for communion, nurturing, and intuitive action has never been more needed than now, as we strive to meet the diverse cultural and environmental challenges of our times. Patriarchy, hierarchy, and obedience to a higher authority all have run their historical course. Governments, families, and businesses built on these unyielding principles of organization are toppling, giving way to more elastic feminine forms of cooperation, communication, and wholeness.

Many American women, however, feel they are losing their hard-won rights, as represented by the nonpassage of ERA, the backlash against freedom of choice in abortion, the slow pace of economic gains, and inequalities in education. But history has shown that real change, fundamental social change, takes many decades or even centuries to become culturally established. Women sometimes may appear to be losing ground, but I believe that the individual woman is stronger and freer than ever, and in a position to greatly influence the course of history.

Setbacks that discourage can be viewed as fresh opportunities to speak up and continue to address not only women's issues, but fundamental human issues. We can welcome these challenges as new platforms for change. Freedom is not easily won, and must be fought for courageously daily, as any member of an underclass will testify. Because of the speed of technological change and the pace of modern life, we expect all change to come quickly, yet perhaps this is an unrealistic expectation. More patience will be required for the vital "woman's work" yet to be done.

Our challenging times reflect the need for women's special gifts. This collection of wisdom offers perspective, courage, and inspiration to women as they continue to shape the world in important ways.

Carol Spenard LaRusso
Novato, California, 1992

Note: The excerpts in the text are followed by the author names; for fictional entries, book titles are also added. Information on more than seventy-five women contributors is found in the alphabetical bibliographic index at the end of the book.

The Wisdom of Women

1

Life and Living

"What then shall I do this morning? How we spend our days is, of course, how we spend our lives. What we do with this hour, and that one, is what we are doing. A schedule defends from chaos and whim. It is a net for catching days."

ANNIE DILLARD

But warm, eager, living life—to be rooted in life—to learn, to desire to know, to feel, to think, to act. That is what I want. And nothing else. That is what I must try for.

KATHERINE MANSFIELD

Your body is the ground metaphor of your life, the expression of your existence. . . . So many of us are not in our bodies, really at home and vibrantly present there. Nor are we in touch with the basic rhythms that constitute our bodily life. We live outside ourselves—in our heads, our memories, our longings—absentee landlords of our own estate.

My way back into life was ecstatic dance. I reentered my body by learning to move my self, to dance my own dance from the inside out, not the outside in.

GABRIELLE ROTH

When any one of us says: "I will live tomorrow," he indulges in a dangerous fantasy about living. The life that the dawn brings us is the only life we have. Life is in the here and now, not in the there and afterwards. The day, with all the travail and joy that it brings to our doorstep, is the expression of eternal life. Either we meet it, we live it—or we miss it.

VIMALA THAKAR

I have picked flowers where I found them— have picked up sea shells and rocks and pieces of wood where there were sea shells and rocks and pieces of wood that I liked. . . . When I found the beautiful white bones on the desert I picked them up and took them home

4

too. . . . I have used these things to say what is to me the wideness and wonder of the world as I live in it.

GEORGIA O'KEEFFE

I want to live only for ecstasy. Small doses, moderate loves, all half-shades, leave me cold. I like extravagance. Letters which give the postman a stiff back to carry, books which overflow from their covers, sexuality which bursts the thermometers.

ANAÏS NIN

Fortunately [psycho]analysis is not the only way to resolve inner conflicts. Life itself still remains a very effective therapist.

KAREN HORNEY

Happiness does not ignore problems and handicaps, but enjoys provocative points of view about them. A problem is a goal that has

manifested in your life, except you don't re-
member asking for it. A handicap is simply an
asset you haven't figured out how to use yet.

ROBERTA JEAN BRYANT

I'll match my flops with anybody's but I
wouldn't have missed 'em. Flops are a part of
life's menu and I've never been a girl to miss
out on any of the courses.

ROSALIND RUSSELL

We cannot write in water. We cannot carve in
water. Water's nature is to flow. And that is
how we should treat negative emotion. When
it comes, let it go. Let it flow away from you
like water moving down a river bed.

How is this different from covering up an
emotion? You acknowledge that you are feeling it, but immediately let it flow through and
away from you. You do not deny it, but you do
release it.

TAE YUN KIM

It is not our circumstances that create our discontent or contentment. It is us.

VIVIAN GREENE

"Have regular hours for work and play; make each day both useful and pleasant, and prove that you understand the worth of time by employing it well. Then youth will be delightful, old age will bring few regrets, and life will become a beautiful success, in spite of poverty."

LOUISA MAY ALCOTT, *Little Women*

Your nutrition can determine how you look, act, and feel; whether you are grouchy or cheerful, homely or beautiful, physiologically and even psychologically young or old; whether you think clearly or are confused, enjoy your work or make it a drudgery, increase your earning power or stay in an economic rut. The foods you eat can make the difference between your day ending with freshness which lets you enjoy a delightful evening or with exhaustion which forces you to bed with the chickens.

ADELLE DAVIS

That which seems hard, "bad luck" on the surface, can be a hidden blessing. . . . We judge life's gifts by their covering and cast them away as ugly, heavy, or hard, missing the love and wisdom that those gifts contain. Life is a generous giver—let's not throw those gifts away unopened.

PAULA PAYNE HARDIN

The mistakes that we male and female mortals make when we have our own way might fairly raise some wonder that we are so fond of it.

GEORGE ELIOT, *Middlemarch*

How can you say luck and chance are the same thing? Chance is the first step you take, luck is what comes afterward. . . . Of course, everything is connected.

AMY TAN, *The Kitchen God's Wife*

I am learning that if I just go on accepting the framework for life that others have given me, if I fail to make my own choices, the reason for my life will be missing. I will be unable to recognize that which I have the power to change. I refuse to spend my life regretting the things I failed to do.

LIV ULLMAN

Learn appreciation. Be willing to take lovingly each small gift of life and receive it and acknowledge that you have received it, and appreciate it and allow it in. You won't be happy with more until you're happy with what you've got.

VIKI KING

When life becomes a process, the old distinctions between winning and losing, success and failure, fade away. Everything, even a negative outcome, has the potential to teach us and to further our quest. . . . In the wider paradigm there are no "enemies," only those useful, if irritating, people whose opposition calls attention to trouble spots, like a magnifying mirror.

MARILYN FERGUSON

I move through my day-to-day life with a sense of appreciation and gratitude that comes from knowing how fortunate I truly am and how unearned all that I am thankful for really is. To have this perspective in my everyday consciousness is in itself a gift, for it leads to feeling "graced," or blessed, each time.

JEAN SHINODA BOLEN

2

Work and Prosperity

"When you are doing the work you love, all else in life seems to fall into place. When you do well in your life's work—whatever that is—you feel well. Your sense of personal worth is keen, and you then see the personal worth of others. It is through the dignity of the work we do that we achieve self-esteem in life."

NANCY ANDERSON

I want to *work*. At what? I want so to live that I may work with my hands and my feeling and my brain. I want a garden, a small house, grass, animals, books, pictures, music. And out of this, the expression of this, I want to be writing. (Though I may write about cabmen. That's no matter.)

KATHERINE MANSFIELD

Virginia Woolf said it beautifully: "Every woman must have a room of her own." I like to carry this one step further. To my way of thinking, every woman must be financially independent, with a nice bank account of her own. Then she can have as many rooms as she likes.

SUZANNE BRANGHAM

One sees the human significance of work—not merely as the means of biological survival, but as the giver of self and the transcender of self, as the creator of human identity and human evolution. . . . Those who have most fully realized themselves, in a sense that can be recognized by the human mind even though it cannot be clearly defined, have done so in the service of a human purpose larger than themselves.

BETTY FRIEDAN

I get out my work and have a show for myself before I have it publicly. I make up my own mind about it—how good or bad or indifferent it is. After that the critics can write what they please. I have already settled it for myself so flattery and criticism go down the same drain and I am quite free.

GEORGIA O'KEEFFE

The difference between an old woman and an elderly lady—so the saying goes—is money. On the assumption that women would prefer to become, in the ripeness of time, elderly ladies, I began advising them some years ago on how to manage money . . . an attempt to inoculate a nation of women to keep them financially healthy.

MARY ELIZABETH SCHLAYER

I am convinced that we become what we do. If our work is stimulating and rewarding, if it pushes us to grow in understanding and knowledge, we become more valuable human beings and relish not only our work, but the other facets of our lives. But if our work is belittling and stressful, if it provides little or no fulfillment, offers no sense of participation, this can have a negative effect. In time, our full

15

human potential will simply shrivel up and we may not even be aware that it is happening.

JANE FONDA

So what's in my future? I don't know, except that I'm going to have another career. . . . I want to move on to another area where my experience can be put to use and my brain can be presented with fresh challenges. . . . I only know that I've always tried to go a step past wherever people expected me to end up. I'm not about to change now.

BEVERLY SILLS

"Don't you feel that it is pleasanter to help one another, to have daily duties which make leisure sweet when it comes, and to bear and forbear, that home may be comfortable and love to us all?"

"We do, mother, we do!" cried the girls.

"Then let me advise you to take up your little burdens again; for though they seem heavy sometimes, they are good for us, and lighten as we learn to carry them. Work is wholesome, and there is plenty for everyone; it keeps us from ennui and mischief, is good for health and spirits, and gives us a sense of power and independence better than money or fashion."

LOUISA MAY ALCOTT, *Little Women*

The fundamental conflict between my sense of myself as a woman and my identity as a scientist could only be resolved by transcending all stereotypical definitions of self and success. . . . It meant establishing a personal identity secure enough to allow me to begin to liberate myself from everyone's labels—including my own. The tension between "woman" and "scientist" is not now so much a source of personal struggle as a profound concern. . . . I hope that the political awareness generated by the women's movement can and will support young women who today attempt to challenge the dogma, still very much alive, that certain kinds of thought are the prerogative of men.

EVELYN FOX KELLER

There is one social skill that can serve as your strongest asset in a job interview. In private life, it makes people fall in love with you and seek you for purposes ranging from honored dinner guest to spouse; and in business it helps more than any other single qualification, with the possible exception of being the owner's eldest child. That is enthusiasm. A look of vitality and happiness, an interest in the world and an eagerness to participate in life, is what is called charm in the social milieu; but in the working world it is called competence.

JUDITH MARTIN

The competitive edge in the coming decades will be held by those individuals and companies who can tap into new, life-driven sources of inspiration, creativity, and vitality.

CAROL ORSBORN

This is a new age—the age of the Prospering Woman. Every day we are breaking more role barriers, and allowing ourselves to think independently about who we are and what success means to us. . . . Prosperity means experiencing balance in life, attaining what we want on mental, physical, emotional, spiritual, and financial levels. Prosperity is the natural result of opening our minds to our creative imaginations and being willing to act on our ideas.

RUTH ROSS

Contemporary feminists have done much to puncture stereotypes, to encourage the rethinking of sex roles and relationships, to work for change in the education of girls, and to open up the question of women's work by insisting on equal pay and equal opportunity.

At present, we insist that a woman be treated just the same as a man. Are we sure we want to be treated as most men are in our society? Or do both sexes deserve something better?

KAY KEESHAN HAMOD

Am I a human being only through my work? Is there something I give in acting that I am unable to possess as a private person—allowing others, through me, to recognize what they have known before?

My work should be the way I live. Thus my life is my work. But roles do not change me; life does.

LIV ULLMAN

Women are forever looking back to see how far they've come, and that interrupts their progress. By this procedure they can have honorable careers, but not accomplish great things. What woman essentially lacks today for doing great things is forgetfulness of herself; but to forget oneself it is first of all necessary to be firmly assured that now and for the future one has found oneself.

SIMONE DE BEAUVOIR

3

Love

"You may know the pains of possessing and dependency, reducing persons to objects, but this is not love. Love doesn't attempt to bind, ensnare, capture. It is light, free of the burden of attachments. Love asks nothing, is fulfilled in itself. When love is there, nothing remains to be done."

VIMALA THAKAR

Only love heals, makes whole, takes us beyond ourselves. Love—not necessarily mushy sentiment or docile passivity—is both right motive and right result. Love gets us There. . . .

MARSHA SINETAR

It is only pride and selfishness and coldness that keep us from having compassion. When we ultimately go home to God, we are going to be judged on what we were to each other, what we did for each other, and, especially, how much love we put in that. It's not how much we give, but how much love we put in the doing—that's compassion in action.

MOTHER TERESA

"Love him? There is nothing left to love."

"There is always something left to love. And if you ain't learned that, you ain't learned nothing. Have you cried for that boy today? . . . What he been through and what it done to him. Child, when do you think is the time to love somebody the most; when they done good and made things easy for everybody? Well then, you ain't through learning—because that ain't the time at all. It's when he's at his lowest and can't believe in hisself 'cause the world done whipped him so. When you starts measuring somebody, measure him right, child, measure him right. Make sure you done taken into account what hills and valleys he come through before he got to wherever he is."

LORRAINE HANSBERRY, *A Raisin in the Sun*

Giving is the highest expression of our power.

VIVIAN GREENE

According to very old wisdom, self-discovery inevitably involves the awakening of the traits usually associated with the opposite sex. All of the gifts of the human mind are available to the conscious self: nurturance and independence, sensitivity and strength. If we complete such qualities within ourselves, we are not as dependent on others for them. Much of what has been labeled love in our culture is infatuation with, and the need for, our missing inner halves.

MARILYN FERGUSON

Love has nothing to do with what you are expecting to get—only with what you are expecting to give—which is everything.

What you will receive in return varies. But it really has no connection with what you give. You give because you love and you cannot help giving. If you are very lucky, you may be loved back. That is delicious but it does not necessarily happen.

KATHARINE HEPBURN

We need first and foremost to learn to love our own experiences and our own process. Learn to accept your own personality for everything that it feels, including anger, hatred, selfishness, judgmentalness, and all the other things that you feel as part of the human experience. You can love other people only to the degree that you've come to love and accept yourself.

SHAKTI GAWAIN

Try this the next time you're between soul mates. Have a love affair with yourself. All that you wish to have outside yourself, cultivate within yourself. If you want somebody who can pick the restaurant, you read the restaurant reviews and pick the restaurant. Take yourself to a movie and enjoy your own company. Be fascinated with yourself. Until you can have a love affair with you, you can't begin to have as much fun as there is with somebody else.

The fact is unalterable that a fellow-mortal with whose nature you are acquainted solely through the brief entrances and exits of a few imaginative weeks called courtship may, when seen in the continuity of married companionship, be disclosed as something better or worse than what you have preconceived, but will certainly not appear altogether the same.

GEORGE ELIOT, *Middlemarch*

I know what it is to live entirely for and with what I love best on earth. I hold myself supremely blessed—blessed beyond what language can express, because I am my husband's life as fully as he is mine. . . . I know no weariness of my Edward's society—he knows none of mine, any more than we each do of the pulsation of the heart that beats in our separate bosoms; consequently, we are ever together. To be together is for us to be at once as free as in solitude, as gay as in company.

CHARLOTTE BRONTË, *Jane Eyre*

There is only one happiness in life, to love and be loved.

GEORGE SAND

"Don't wait for it [love]," I said. "Create a world, your world. Alone. Stand alone. Create. And then the love will come to you, then it comes to you. It was only when I wrote my first book that the world I wanted to live in opened to me."

ANAÏS NIN

Only when we truly reveal ourselves can we ever be truly loved. When we relate as we genuinely are, from our essence, then if we are loved it is our essence that is loved. Nothing is more validating on a personal level, and more freeing in a relationship. It must be noted, however, that this kind of behavior on our part is only possible in a climate that is free of fear, so we must not only conquer our own fears of being genuine but also avoid people whose attitudes and behaviors toward us produce fear.

ROBIN NORWOOD

"For six years now I have gone around by myself and built up my science. And now I am a master. Son, I can love anything. No longer do I have to think about it even. I see a street full of people and a beautiful light comes in me. I watch a bird in the sky. Or I meet a traveler on the road. Everything, Son. And anybody. All strangers and all loved! Do you realize what a science like mine can mean?"

CARSON MC CULLERS,
The Ballad of the Sad Café

4

Freedom

*"People always say that I didn't give up
my seat [to a white man] because I was
tired, but that isn't true. I was not
physically tired, or no more tired than I
usually was at the end of a working day.
. . . No, the only tired I was, was tired of
giving in."*

ROSA PARKS

How can you hesitate? Risk! Risk anything!
Care no more for the opinion of others, for
those voices. Do the hardest thing on earth for
you. Act for yourself. Face the truth.

KATHERINE MANSFIELD

I hung on the wall the work I had been doing
for several months. Then I sat down and
looked at it. I could see how each painting or
drawing had been done according to one
teacher or another, and I said to myself, "I
have things in my head that are not like what

anyone has taught me—shapes and ideas so near to me—so natural to my way of being and thinking that it hasn't occurred to me to put them down." I decided to start anew—to strip away what I had been taught—to accept as true my own thinking.

GEORGIA O'KEEFFE

It seems that the older the teaching, the more it presents self-wisdom and self-honor as a source of strength, rebellion, and a kind of meta-democracy—a oneness with all living things and with the universe itself. Returning to this concept of circularity and oneness that preceded patriarchy, racism, class systems, and other hierarchies that ration self-esteem—and that create obedience to external authority by weakening belief in our natural and internal wisdom—is truly a revolution from within.

GLORIA STEINEM

Only human beings living in freedom can create a new society, a new dimension of love and consciousness in which the tenderness of love and compassion can flower in each human heart.

VIMALA THAKAR

Women are never supposed to have any occupation of sufficient importance *not* to be interrupted, except suckling; . . . and women themselves have accepted this, have written books to support it, and have trained themselves so as to consider whatever they do as *not* of such value to the world or to others, but that they can throw it up at the first "claim of social life." They have accustomed themselves to consider intellectual occupation as a merely selfish amusement, which it is their "duty" to give up for every trifler more selfish than themselves.

FLORENCE NIGHTINGALE

My belief is that if we live another century or so—I am talking of the common life which is the real life and not of the little separate lives which we live as individuals—and have five hundred [English pounds] a year each of us and rooms of our own; if we have the habit of freedom and the courage to write exactly what we think; . . . that we go alone and that our relation is to the world of reality and not only to the world of men and women, then the opportunity will come and the dead poet who was Shakespeare's sister will put on the body which she has often laid down. Drawing her life from the lives of the unknown who were her forerunners, as her brother did before her, she will be born.

VIRGINIA WOOLF

"I am sure, sir, I should never mistake informality for insolence; one I rather like, the other nothing free-born would submit to, even for a salary."

CHARLOTTE BRONTË, *Jane Eyre*

Women must leave off asking [men] and being influenced by them, but retire within themselves, and explore the ground-work of life till they find their peculiar secret. Then, when they come forth again, renovated and baptized, they will know how to turn all dross to gold, and will be rich and free though they live in a hut, tranquil if in a crowd. Then their sweet singing shall not be from passionate impulse, but the lyrical overflow of a divine rapture, and a new music shall be evolved from this many-chorded world.

MARGARET FULLER

I was a slave in the state of New York; and now I am a good citizen of this state. . . . I come forth to speak about Woman's Rights, and want to throw in my little mite, to keep the scales a-movin'. I know that it feels a kind o' hissin' and ticklin' like to see a colored woman get up and tell you about things, and Woman's Rights. We have all been thrown down so low that nobody thought we'd ever get up again; but we have been long enough trodden now; we will come up again.

Now, women do not ask half of a kingdom,

but their rights, and they don't get 'em. . . .
But we'll have our rights; see if we don't, and
you can't stop us from them. You may hiss as
much as you like, but it is comin'. . . . I am
above eighty years old; it is about time for me
to be going. I have been forty years a slave and
forty years free, and would be here forty years
more to have equal rights for all. I suppose I
am kept here because something remains for
me to do.

SOJOURNER TRUTH

For three centuries they [actresses, dancers,
and singers] have been almost the only women
to maintain a concrete independence in the
midst of society, and at the present time they
still occupy a privileged place in it. Formerly
actresses were anathema to the Church, and
the very excessiveness of that severity has always authorized a great freedom of behavior
on their part. . . . Like courtesans, they spend
a great deal of their time in the company of
men; but making their own living and finding

the meaning of their lives in their work, they escape the yoke of men.

SIMONE DE BEAUVOIR

"What does freedom mean?" a man from the unofficial [Polish] press asked me. Perhaps there are two kinds of freedom, I said. The kind that is born into and taken for granted, like mine in the States; and the kind measured by the little victories of its acquisition, each one savored and celebrated.

At home [in America] we have freedom of speech, but fewer and fewer words with any meaning are ever spoken. We have freedom of thought, but nothing pushes us toward creative thinking. We have freedom of choice, and a diminishing quality of moral and spiritual values characterizing our choices. And here, where you have to fight for it, a spirit is created. . . . The people sing, cherish their children, love their church, and care for their neighbors.

JOAN BAEZ

Trusting that larger forces than yourself are at work in your life, you will give up the demand for the outcome you think you want and learn to appreciate whatever it is you get. This is true freedom.

CAROL ORSBORN

If we are to achieve a richer culture, rich in contrasting values, we must recognize the whole gamut of human potentialities, and so weave a less arbitrary social fabric, one in which each diverse human gift will find a fitting place.

MARGARET MEAD

5

War and Peace

"There has been a saying, 'Well, we'll always have war.' My answer is, 'We will not always have war. We will always have conflict.' What we need is to learn to use conflict creatively, to grow and to help other people grow in the process, and to work out a better solution than could possibly be thought of alone."

KATHARINE WHITESIDE TAYLOR

Patriarchy is commonly understood as meaning domination and control. Thus nuclear weapons are the ideal patriarchal weapons because of their immense capacity to dominate, control, and destroy. However, they are also a woman's issue because the recognition of the connectedness of life is a woman's recognition. I don't subscribe to the idea that war is strictly a masculine invention, though historically this has been true; but there is a danger in looking at the situation that way and viewing women as nurturers and men as destroyers. It ultimately implies inequality between the sexes. I have met destructive women and nurturing men in my life and know that both exist.

DIANE THOMAS

With regard to the sexual connotations of words, can we all not think of what a dream will be realized for the race when the noun "soldier," for example, ceases to conjure up romantic notions of masculinity, but will instead have been unsexed and (at long last) put in its true place in history by the more accurate associations it recalls: "tragedy . . . the organized waste of human life and potential"?

LORRAINE HANSBERRY

The numbers games of analysts are a distraction from the real issue of the survival of the human race. Women come to the nuclear movement understanding in their hearts and minds that survival is the primary issue. We

come to it with love and power. If we harness
that power, we will change the world.

PATRICIA ELLSBERG

I find patriotism not only a refuge of scoun-
drels but of idiots and those who like to buy
their thinking ready-made each morning in
the vacuous newspapers. Every decade or so
governments create wars and whip up a
frenzy, so that we will not notice the short-
comings of our own side and will not question
the assumptions of our society and demand
more rational institutions and laws.

MARGE PIERCY, *Gone to Soldiers*

The work of activists, citizen groups, teachers,
physicians, lawyers, labor unions, neighbor-
hood associations, church groups, and many
others has cleared a path through the dense
jungle of the nuclear threat. Now there is a
road there, and it is being paved. But we
must not let these signs of civilization lull us
into quiet reassurance. That road's direction is

45

not clear; to ensure continued progress will take constant vigilance.

CHRISTINE K. CASSEL

How do we know the button isn't being pressed right now, or a computer hasn't made a mistake and the [nuclear] weapons are on their way? . . . We practice psychic numbing. We don't want to think about it and so we don't. . . . The therapy is us. We can all be as powerful as the most powerful person on the planet. . . . We were put here to save the planet and no other generation has had such a responsibility placed on its shoulders. That's why we are here.

HELEN CALDICOTT

We need to take a leap of the imagination and envision nations as the best kinds of families: the democratic ones we are trying to create in our own lives. A hierarchical family must be changed anyway if we are to stop producing leaders whose unexamined early lives are then played out on a national and international stage. . . . Changing the way we raise children is the only long-term path to peace or arms control, and neither has ever been more crucial. As the feminist adage says, *The personal is political.*

GLORIA STEINEM

The opportunity that the bomb presents us with can be discussed in the sense of a spiritual teaching in that for the first time in history there is no private salvation. There is no place to hide.

This does something to the way we see ourselves and each other. We need to find enlightenment inside ourselves, with all our pains and failures and sense of confusion. We can't take time to spend three years in a cave in the Himalayas. We have to find enlightenment now.

JOANNA MACY

The women's movement is essential to the disarmament movement, because we learned from that how the process by which we promote social change creates the kind of society we will then have. We need to avoid the problems of hierarchy, domination, and egoism that play into many of the progressive movements in this country.

It's not enough just to disarm. Without changing the structure of society, we will continue to perpetuate warfare or other forms of repression or control that cause suffering. We cannot change society until we change ourselves.

ELEANOR LE CAIN

The more we learn about the life of the peoples of our countries today, their concerns and their aspirations, the sooner we will have a better understanding of one another. . . . Quite a number of differences stand between us. But I feel that they in no way hinder discussions of any problems that are of concern to us: how to preserve peace, how to make the life of every individual on earth worthy of our times.

RAISA GORBACHEV

World peace is *us*. . . . We are each walking agents of the vision of peace we carry inside us.

KATHLEEN VANDE KIEFT

6

The Human Family

"The wider paradigm of relationships and family transcends old group definitions. The discovery of our connection to all other men, women, and children joins us to another family. Indeed, seeing ourselves as a planetary family struggling to solve its problems, rather than as assorted people and nations assessing blame or exporting solutions, could be the ultimate shift in perspective."

MARILYN FERGUSON

Woman must be still as the axis of a wheel in the midst of her activities; . . . she must be the pioneer in achieving this stillness, not only for her own salvation, but for the salvation of family life, of society, perhaps even of our civilization.

ANNE MORROW LINDBERGH

The need for connection and contact between human beings is very important to acknowledge. Not only do we need intimate relationships with our partners, nuclear families, and close friends, but we also need a sense of connectedness to an extended family, tribe, or community. We need to have a feeling of belonging to a larger group. Ultimately, we need to feel that we are part of the whole human family and connected to all beings on earth.

SHAKTI GAWAIN

Because of their age-long training in human relations—for that is what feminine intuition really is—women have a special contribution to make to any group enterprise, and I feel it is up to them to contribute the kinds of awareness that relatively few men . . . have incorporated through their education.

MARGARET MEAD

Saying no to the feminine mystique and organizing to confront sex discrimination was only the first stage. We have somehow to transcend the polarities of the first stage, and . . . get on to the second stage: the restructuring of our institutions on a basis of real equality for women and men, so we can live a new "yes" to life and love, and can *choose* to have children.

BETTY FRIEDAN

In the old days, the primary job of the native Lakota mother was to teach the new child that he or she was connected with everything in the circle of life. She would take the child walking and say, "See the squirrel? That's your brother. See the tree? We are related. This is your family; these are all your family." Because they were all brought up that way, they knew deeply that they were all interconnected, they were all family, they were all conscious. Lakota children had an opportunity to begin early in life to attend to the whole or the holiness, the spiritual side of things, and then to expand this ability powerfully as they grew.

BROOKE MEDICINE EAGLE

There is no great difference in the reality of one country or another, because it is always people you meet everywhere. They may look different or be dressed differently, or may have a different education or position. But they are all the same. They are all people to be loved. They are all hungry for love.

MOTHER TERESA

Rock 'n' roll has become a universal form of music. It moves beyond boundaries, beyond politics, beyond religion, economics, culture, sociology, language, custom, and ideology. Rock 'n' roll speaks to the soul of freedom. . . . Rock concerts are the modern tribal rituals where communal ecstasy is a real possibility. . . . This is religious experience, holy communion. Our young people are starving for unity and this is their hope.

GABRIELLE ROTH

I've heard it said that what separates men and women from the beasts is that men and women must tell their stories. Our stories unite us with nature and the primitive, bonding us with our own beauty and our own beast.

My story belongs to no one else, and yet

our stories, yours and mine, are the same un-
der the skin, beyond the facts, beyond the
names and dates. Only the heart speaks to the
heart. . . . I needed to tell you my story as I
need to hear yours, so that we may share our
secrets and trust our hearts.

JUDY COLLINS

7

Our Earth and Future

"Because we have been out of touch with our own spirit, we have been out of touch with our natural environment. We have been in conflict with nature rather than in harmony with her. In fact, we have seen ourselves as the conquerors of the earth. Now we must recognize that we have been entrusted with the stewardship of the planet. We are the caretakers of the earth."

SHAKTI GAWAIN

We are living in a time when we have new powers never dreamed of by our ancestors. . . . We can alter DNA, the delicate genetic coding that has built up through centuries of natural selection. In the next two decades, we can literally determine the fate of 500,000 to one million plant and animal species. They may go out of existence because of human decisions, and even God will not be able to bring them back. And we can literally eliminate all life on Earth through our weapons of mass destruction.

We have new powers over life and death, and therefore we are called to take on new responsibilities for the uses of these powers. We are entering the adult phase of human evolution. We must become wiser, more spiritual human beings, more deeply attuned to the earth processes than we've ever been before.

PATRICIA MISCHE

It took hundreds of millions of years to produce the life that now inhabits the earth—eons in which that developing and evolving and diversifying life reached a state of adjustment and balance with its surroundings. The environment, rigorously shaping and directing the life it supported, contained elements that were hostile as well as supporting. Given time—time not in years but in millennia—life adjusts, and a balance has been reached. For time is the essential ingredient; but in the modern world there is no time.

RACHEL CARSON

North American Indians are the third or fourth largest producers of uranium in the world. We ended up on reservations, on land everyone thought was worthless. This was our sacred land, a great deal of which we have retained rights to. The land that has the power of sacred creation also has the power of imminent destruction.

The issue is one of respect for the land, for other people, and for creation. If we relearn that respect and are humble knowing we are no greater or better than anything else, then we will have learned something that we can bring to our work and to our way of life. When we lose our respect, we allow the abuse of the Earth and forget that it is related to us.

WINONA LA DUKE

For a brief period in Greece, East and West met; the bias toward the rational that was to distinguish the West, and the deep spiritual inheritance of the East were united. The full effect of this meeting [shows] the immense stimulus to creative activity when clarity of mind is added to spiritual power. . . .

It is worth our while in the confusions and bewilderments of the present to consider the way by which the Greeks arrived at the clarity of their thought and the affirmation of their art. Very different conditions of life confronted them from those we face, but it is ever to be borne in mind that though the outside of human life changes much, the inside changes little, and the lesson-book we cannot graduate from is human experience.

EDITH HAMILTON

8

Growing Older

"Perhaps middle age is, or should be, a period of shedding shells; the shell of ambition, the shell of material accumulations and possessions, the shell of the ego. Perhaps one can shed at this stage in life as one sheds in beach-living; one's pride, one's false ambitions, one's mask, one's armor. Was that armor not put on to protect one from the competitive world? If one ceases to compete, does one need it? Perhaps one can at last in middle age, if not earlier, be completely oneself. And what a liberation that would be!"

ANNE MORROW LINDBERGH

How dissatisfied I was with the idea that Life must be a lesser thing than we were capable of imagining it to be. I had the feeling that the same thing happened to nearly everybody I knew and whom I did not know. No sooner was their youth . . . done, than they stopped growing. At the very moment that one felt now was the time to gather oneself together, to use one's whole strength, to take control, to be an adult, in fact, they seemed content to swap the darling wish of their hearts for innumerable little wishes.

KATHERINE MANSFIELD

Miss Manners detects an unpleasant suggestion that while being very young or very old is considered fetching, being fully grown-up is not, particularly for women. Our most usual form of flattery is to tell people that they look much younger than they are, such compliments often being supported in the most ludicrous fashion. How discouraging to think that the natural progress of life is downhill. . . . Miss Manners has found that age does bring change, but its chief movement seems to be in the direction of sense.

JUDITH MARTIN

Time is not a line but a dimension, like the dimensions of space. . . . I began then to think of time as having a shape, something you could see, like a series of liquid transparencies, one laid on top of another. You don't look back along time but down through it, like water. Sometimes this comes to the surface, sometimes that, sometimes nothing. Nothing goes away.

MARGARET ATWOOD, *Cat's Eye*

Midlife brings with it an invitation to accept ourselves as we truly are, embracing the darker sides of ourselves as well as the good, the dark sides of our cultures as well as the good. We have an instinctive fear of facing the dark mysteries. The shadow or unknown parts of us belong to an inner world that is usually suppressed in the first half of life. . . . But by confronting our mysterious and shadowy center, we tap into life's revitalizing energies and gain access to our innermost self, which contains the key to a new understanding of our life's meaning.

PAULA PAYNE HARDIN

I don't believe for a minute that you can hang on to your youth. I think it's the worst, the saddest, the most futile struggle. I know a lot of women who've gone through cosmetic surgery, and it shows in photographs, something strange happens around the mouth. . . . I've had enough trouble trying to stay myself, be myself. It's something you have to work at just as hard as you'd have to work at staying young.

ROSALIND RUSSELL

Maturity involves the synthesis of all you've learned. It's the time of the soul, the essence of all you are. As adolescence unleashed the mind, childhood the heart, and the birth cycle the body, maturity brings out the soul. The keys to maturity are commitment and responsibility.

It's time to stop studying, stop preparing, stop searching and to start teaching, doing, manifesting, producing. The rehearsals are over, the show is on.

GABRIELLE ROTH

For women who have awakened to new possibilities in middle age, or who were born into the current women's movement and have escaped the usual rhythms of the once traditional female existence, the last third of life is likely to require new attitudes and new courage.

CAROLYN G. HEILBRUN

During much of the feminist movement women redesigned themselves as men and disregarded their greatest gifts—openmindedness, flexibility, intuition. Now they are ridding themselves of stereotypes and cultural myths and tuning in to what it really means to be a woman—seeing menopause as a sacred rite of passage, for example. Women are taking their gifts seriously, to gently persuade, to gently be leaders.

MARILYN MC GUIRE

9

The Human Spirit

"The best and most beautiful things in the world cannot be seen or even touched. They must be felt with the heart."

HELEN KELLER

There is a feeling of absolute finality about the end of a flight through darkness. The whole scheme of things with which you have lived acutely, during hours of roaring sound in an element altogether detached from the world, ceases abruptly. . . . The dream of flight is suddenly gone before the mundane realities of growing grass and swirling dust, the slow plodding of men and the enduring patience of rooted trees. Freedom escapes you again, and wings that were a moment ago no less than an eagle's, and swifter, are metal and wood once more, inert and heavy.

BERYL MARKHAM

Nothing in life is trivial. Life is whole wherever and whenever we touch it, and one moment or event is not less sacred than another.

VIMALA THAKAR

There is no shortage of good days. It is good lives that are hard to come by. A life of good days lived in the senses is not enough. The life of sensation is the life of greed; it requires more and more. The life of the spirit requires less and less; time is ample and its passage sweet.

ANNIE DILLARD

How come we've got these bodies? They are frail supports for what we feel. There are times I get so hemmed in by my arms and legs I look forward to getting past them. As though death will set me free like a traveling cloud. . . . I'll be out there as a piece of the endless body of the world feeling pleasures so much larger than skin and bones and blood.

LOUISE ERDRICH, *Love Medicine*

Relationship is probably the most powerful spiritual path that exists in the world today.

It's the greatest tool that we have. Our relationships can be the fastest and the most powerful route to the deepest truth, if we know how to use them.

SHAKTI GAWAIN

"Who then," she continues, "tells a finer tale than any of us? Silence does. And where does one read a deeper tale than upon the most perfectly printed page of the most precious book? Upon the blank page. When a royal and gallant pen, in the moment of its highest inspiration, has written down its tale with the rarest ink of all—where, then, may one read a still deeper, sweeter, merrier and more cruel tale than that? Upon the blank page."

ISAK DINESEN, *Last Tales*

Great literature, past or present, is the expression of great knowledge of the human heart; great art is the expression of a solution of the conflict between the demands of the world without and that within.

EDITH HAMILTON

Art for art's sake is an empty phrase. Art for the sake of the true, art for the sake of the good and the beautiful, that is the faith I am searching for.

GEORGE SAND

And who *are* you? Are you simply that person of flesh and blood who stands before you in the mirror every day? Or are you more—much more—than you ever dreamed possible? That connection within is your lifeline to unlimited possibility. It is the thread that will lead you to the wonders and mysteries of infinite vision. It is the cord connecting you to your ultimate path of power. It can lift you up and move you far beyond the mediocrity of your assumptions about yourself.

KATHLEEN VANDE KIEFT

To achieve greatness, you must be willing to surrender ambition.

CAROL ORSBORN

The power to live a full, adult, living, breathing life in close contact with what I love — the earth and the wonders thereof, the sea, the sun . . . . I want to enter into it, to be part of it, to live in it, to learn from it, to lose all that is superficial and acquired in me, and to become a conscious direct human being. I want, by understanding myself, to understand others. I want to be all that I am capable of becoming. . . .

KATHERINE MANSFIELD

I feel no need for any other faith than my faith in human beings. Like Confucius of old, I am so absorbed in the wonder of earth and the life upon it that I cannot think of heaven and the angels. I have enough for this life. If there is no other life, then this one has been enough to

79

make it worth being born, myself a human being.

PEARL S. BUCK

When we experience moments of ecstasy—in play, in stillness, in art, in sex—they come not as an exception, an accident, but as a taste of what life is meant to be. . . . Ecstasy is an idea, a goal, but it can be the expectation of every day. Those times when we're grounded in our body, pure in our heart, clear in our mind, rooted in our soul, and suffused with the energy, the spirit of life, are our birthright. It's really not that hard to stop and luxuriate in the joy and wonder of being. Children do it all the time. It's a natural human gift that should be at the heart of our lives.

GABRIELLE ROTH

But my life, any life, real life, wasn't about pursuing the prizes of materialism and practicing the gospel of self-gratification. Life was about enduring adversity, about being true to oneself, about striving to do the will of one's Creator so that one could live in harmony with all that was finest in one's nature. The real prizes were not. . . . health, wealth and happiness, that facile trio which could be destroyed so easily by the first breath of misfortune, but faith, hope and, above all, love.

SUSAN HOWATCH, *Ultimate Prizes*

You gain strength, courage, and confidence by every experience in which you really stop to look fear in the face. You are able to say to yourself, "I lived through this horror. I can take the next thing that comes along." . . . You must do the thing you think you cannot do.

ELEANOR ROOSEVELT

I will fight anyone who will take us back to the days of darkness.

BARBARA BOXER

The twentieth century will not close without the presence of women being felt.

BARBARA JORDAN

It is never too late to be what you might have been.

GEORGE ELIOT

About the Editor

Carol Spenard LaRusso, formerly an executive editor with New World Library, has taught English and music, and has a B.A. and M.A. in English literature. Born and raised in New York, she moved to San Francisco in 1968, and currently makes her home in Marin County, California, near her two daughters and grand-daughters.

Ms. LaRusso divides her time between writing and music, and is the editor of *The Green Thoreau,* also in the Classic Wisdom Collection.

Bibliographic Index

The information in this index allows the reader to locate the contributions of authors within the text and to further explore their writing. Applicable publisher permissions and copyright notices follow the index.

Nightingale, Florence (1820–1910) English nurse and reformer (*Cassandra*, 1852–59), 35

Nin, Anaïs (1903–1977) French-American writer (*Diary*, Volume One, 1931–1934), 5, 28

Norwood, Robin, American therapist and writer (*Women Who Love Too Much*, 1985), 28–29

O'Keeffe, Georgia (1887–1986) American painter (*Georgia O'Keeffe* [autobiography & art] 1976), 4–5, 14 15, 33–34

Orsborn, Carol, American entrepreneur and writer (*Inner Excellence*, 1992), 18, 40, 79

Parks, Rosa, African-American civil rights leader (*Rosa Parks: My Story*, 1992), 33

Piercy, Marge, American novelist and poet (*Gone to Soldiers*, 1987), 45

Roosevelt, Eleanor (1884–1962) American stateswoman and social reformer (*You Learn by Living*, 1960), 81

Ross, Ruth, American writer (*Prospering Woman*, 1982), 18–19

Roth, Gabrielle, American dancer and teacher (*Maps to Ecstasy*, 1989), 3–4, 56, 70, 80

THE CLASSIC WISDOM COLLECTION
OF
NEW WORLD LIBRARY

As You Think by James Allen. Edited and with an Introduction by Marc Allen. October, 1991.

Native American Wisdom. Compiled and with an Introduction by Kent Nerburn and Louise Mengelkoch. October, 1991.

The Art of True Healing by Israel Regardie. Edited and updated by Marc Allen. October, 1991.

Letters to a Young Poet by Rainer Maria Rilke. Translated by Joan M. Burnham with an Introduction by Marc Allen. April, 1992.

The Green Thoreau. Selected and with an Introduction by Carol Spenard LaRusso. April, 1992.

Political Tales & Truth of Mark Twain. Edited and with an Introduction by David Hodge and Stacey Freeman. November, 1992.

The Wisdom of Women. Selected and with an Introduction by Carol Spenard LaRusso. November, 1992.

New World Library is dedicated to publishing books and cassettes that help improve the quality of our lives.

For a catalog of our fine books and cassettes, contact:

New World Library
58 Paul Drive
San Rafael, CA 91903
Phone: (415) 472-2100
FAX: (415) 472-6131

Or call toll free:

(800) 227-3900
In Calif.: (800) 632-2122